For
Gyro, Theo, and Toby

Copyright © 2011 by Flying Marconi Bros. Entertainment

The type was set in Garamond Semibold 14pt. The illustrations were created with digital acrylics on digital illustration board.

Library of Congress Cataloging-in-Publication Data
Library of Congress Control Number: 2011937299

Marconi, Greg, 1974 & Marconi, Michael, 1971

We Made You Out of Love / Greg Marconi & Michael Marconi; with illustrations by Daniel Han. - 1st ed. p. cm.
Audience: ages 3 & up
Summary: A journey through a child's imagination to answer the age-old question: "Where did I come from?"
Published by Telemachus Press, LLC - www.TelemachusPress.com
ISBN: 978-1-937387-25-9
[1. birth-Fiction. 2. family-Fiction. 3. imaginary friends-Fiction.] I. Marconi, Greg. II. Marconi, Michael. v. Title.

Special thanks to Ellen Marconi, Keith Brauneisen, Kara Morrissette, Lindsey Humphrey, Paul Gregory, Claudia Diaz, Tom Newman and Duy Nguyen.

Check out more high-flying action and suspense at www.FlyingMarconiBros.com

FLYING MARCONI BROS.
ENTERTAINMENT

We Made You Out of Love

The Answer To The Number One Question On Every Child's Mind:

"Where Did I Come From?"

Written by

Dr. Greg Marconi & Michael Marconi

Illustrations by Daniel Han • Art Direction by Jason Marconi

Jeffrey came home from school one day
with a very important question on his mind.

"I want to know where I came from," Jeffrey said.

"Where you came from?"
his mother replied.

"Yes," said Jeffrey.
"I want to know where I came from."

"Did you and Mommy create me?" Jeffrey asked.
"Yes," his father said. "We created you together."

Jeffrey smiled. "Like in a chemistry lab?
With chemicals and smoke and acid and stuff?"

Mommy and Daddy laughed.
"Not quite like that," his mother said.

"Was I hatched from a giant egg?"
asked Jeffrey.

"You did start out as an egg,"
his father explained.

"I bet Mommy sat on me for a whole year until I broke out of my shell with my feathers and claws and my big, colorful dragon wings," Jeffrey growled.

"Not exactly," said Mommy.

"Did Daddy build me?" Jeffrey asked.
"No, I didn't build you," his father replied.

"You should have built me 50 feet tall," Jeffrey whined.
"Then I could breathe fire and smoke and shoot laser beams out of my eyes."

"That sounds like fun," said Mommy.
"But I think I like you just the size you are."

"Did you grow me?" asked Jeffrey.

"Yes," his mother explained. "I grew you for nine whole months."

Jeffrey jumped to his feet and stomped around the room.
"Did I grow in the garden, with flowers for ears,
Venus Flytrap fingers, and vines that shot out of my toes?"

"Vines that shot out of your toes?" Daddy chuckled.
"It wasn't quite like that, but Mommy did grow you."

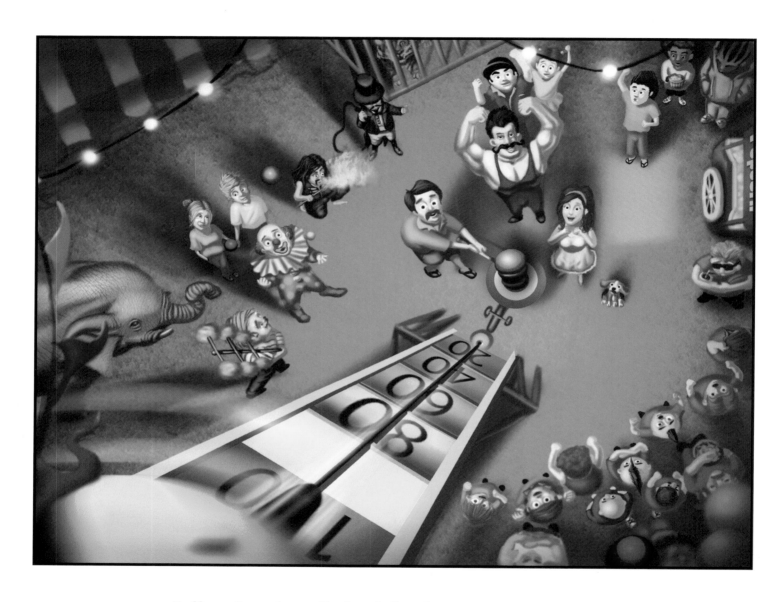

Jeffrey thought really hard. "Did you win me?" he asked.
"Where would we win you?" his mother replied.
"At the carnival," Jeffrey said.

Jeffrey flexed his muscles.
"Daddy rang the bell on the strongman game
and won you a cute little prize."

Mommy and Daddy laughed.
"You would be the cutest prize of all,
but Daddy didn't win you for me," said Mommy.

"Did you find me?" Jeffrey asked.

Daddy smiled. "Where would we find someone as cute as you?"

"In the desert, after my spaceship crash-landed," Jeffrey said.

"I probably had long tentacle arms, three bulging eyes and a mouthful of giant, purple teeth."
Mommy shivered. "Giant, purple teeth sound scary."

Jeffrey giggled.
"Don't be scared, Mommy. I wouldn't have eaten you."
Mommy laughed. "That's good to know, Jeffrey."

"Did I appear in a puff of smoke?" asked Jeffrey.
"You mean, out of thin air?" his mother replied.

"No," said Jeffrey, "out of Daddy's magic hat."

Jeffrey wrapped his blanket around his neck and jumped to his feet.
"The Great Daderino was onstage with his cape and magic wand and said, 'Alakazam,
Hocus-Ka-Pocus, Presto-Ka-Change-o' and then poof, out popped…me!"

"That sounds like a neat trick," said Daddy,
"but that's not quite how it happened."

"Did you and Mommy invent me?" Jeffrey asked.

"How could we invent you?" his father replied.

Jeffrey clenched his teeth and made a scary face.
"In a mad scientist's lab," he said.
You probably even put my feet on backwards."

Mommy giggled. "No, you didn't come from a mad scientist's lab,
and Daddy didn't put your feet on backwards."

"Did you and Daddy make me?" asked Jeffrey.

"Yes," his mother said. "We made you together."

Jeffrey rubbed his belly. "Did you make me in the kitchen, with flour and sugar, and was my hair made out of chocolate sprinkles?"

"Chocolate sprinkles sound delicious," his father said,
"but that's not how we made you."

"Then how did you make me?" Jeffrey asked.
"We made you out of love," his mother replied.
"Out of love?" asked Jeffrey.

"Yes, we made you out of love," his father explained.
"Before you were born, Mommy and I decided that we loved each other so much,
that we wanted something that was part of her and part of me."

Mommy smiled. "We held each other really close and we wished for a little boy or a little girl. You grew in my tummy for nine whole months and I took care of you until the day you were born."

Daddy hugged Mommy. "That was the day we became a family."
"Are you happy you made me?" asked Jeffrey.

"Yes, Jeffrey. You're the best thing we ever made."

CONTRIBUTORS

(left to right: Illustrator Daniel Han , Co-Author Michael Marconi, Co-Author Dr. Greg Marconi, Art Director Jason Marconi)

Dr. Greg Marconi, co-author, is a board-certified pediatrician working in the emergency room of one of the most prestigious children's hospitals in California. He is a fellow of the American Academy of Pediatrics and a clinical instructor at the USC Keck School of Medicine. He is well regarded by both his patients and his peers, and he prides himself on working with parents and children on preventative healthcare and health education. Greg lives, works and snowboards in Southern California.

Michael Marconi, co-author, is a multi-award winning author and filmmaker. He was a finalist for his screenplay "The Perfect Wedding" in the 2005 American Screenplay competition, and his film/video work has been nominated for Cable Ace, Key Art and Emmy awards. Michael is honored to have won a total of 16 Promax and 2 Telly awards for his various marketing and advertising campaigns. When not writing, producing or directing, Michael hangs with his dog Theo and snowboards in Southern California.

Daniel Han, illustrator, is a graduate of Pasadena Art Center College of Design. He is an illustrator and conceptual artist. He has worked on projects such as feature film concept design, digital paintings, video game design, amusement park design, character design, background creation and picture book illustration. When not drawing or painting, Daniel snowboards, plays video games and teaches art to children in Southern California.

Jason Marconi, art director, is an award-winning art director/graphic designer. He has worked on a variety of projects including feature film main title sequences, television promos, commercials, television show main titles, DVD menus and illustrated children's books. He has worked for companies such as Warner Bros., Disney, 20th Century Fox, Sony, E! and MTV. In his spare time, Jason snowboards and surfs in Southern California.

CPSIA information can be obtained
at www.ICGtesting.com
Printed in the USA
255430LV00004BA